HOW TO SHOOT LIKE A
NAVY SEAL

Combat Marksmanship Fundamentals

CHRIS SAJNOG

© 2013 by Center Mass Group, LLC
San Diego, CA 92129
http://centermassgroup.com

Produced in the United States
ISBN: 978-0-9892664-5-1

First Edition:
10 9 8 7 6 5 4 3 2 1

Dedicated to
My two warrior sons, Caden and Owen.

Contents

Navy SEAL Creed

In times of war or uncertainty there is a special breed of warrior ready to answer our Nation's call. A common man with uncommon desire to succeed.

Forged by adversity, he stands alongside America's finest special operations forces to serve his country, the American people, and protect their way of life.

I am that man.

My Trident is a symbol of honor and heritage. Bestowed upon me by the heroes that have gone before, it embodies the trust of those I have sworn to protect. By wearing the Trident I accept the responsibility of my chosen profession and way of life. It is a privilege that I must earn every day.

My loyalty to Country and Team is beyond reproach. I humbly serve as a guardian to my fellow Americans always ready to defend those who are unable to defend themselves. I do not advertise the nature of my work, nor seek recognition for my actions. I voluntarily accept the inherent hazards of my profession, placing the welfare and security of others before my own.

I serve with honor on and off the battlefield. The ability to control my emotions and my actions, regardless of circumstance, sets me apart from other men.

Uncompromising integrity is my standard. My character and honor are steadfast. My word is my bond.

We expect to lead and be led. In the absence of orders I will take charge, lead my teammates and accomplish the mission. I lead by example in all situations.

I will never quit. I persevere and thrive on adversity. My Nation expects me to be physically harder and mentally stronger than my enemies. If knocked down, I will get back up, every time. I will draw on every remaining ounce of strength to protect my teammates and to accomplish our mission. I am never out of the fight.

We demand discipline. We expect innovation. The lives of my teammates and the success of our mission depend on me — my technical skill, tactical proficiency, and attention to detail. My training is never complete.

We train for war and fight to win. I stand ready to bring the full spectrum of combat power to bear in order to achieve my mission and the goals established by my country. The execution of my duties will be swift and violent when required yet guided by the very principles that I serve to defend.

Brave men have fought and died building the proud tradition and feared reputation that I am bound to uphold. In the worst of conditions, the legacy of my teammates steadies my resolve and silently guides my every deed. I will not fail.

Introduction

To be a great shooter you need to seek perfection in everything you do. Unlike many endeavors, shooting is literally either hit or miss. There is no "close enough" when it comes to taking low-percentage shots in a high-stress environment. This means not only a strong foundation in the basics, but performing the basics exceedingly well. It takes Virtuosity.

I was first introduced to the term *virtuosity* back in 2005 in a CrossFit article by Coach Gregg Glassman. He talked about the importance of virtuosity as a CrossFit trainer and used the gymnastics definition of, "performing the common, uncommonly well."

As a Navy SEAL sniper instructor I understood this style of training and had been practicing it for years, but it was not until I saw this article that I had seen it put into words so well. So before I get into the how of combat marksmanship, I want to explain the importance of virtuosity in firearms training and the theory behind my training model.

Becoming a virtuoso of firearms requires hours upon hours of dedication and perseverance. There are no shortcuts to becoming a master, but there is a tendency among new shooters to ignore the basic fundamentals of marksmanship and quickly move to learning more "advanced" or "cool" looking techniques, skills, or added movements. This pattern of novice training is apparent in all kinds of skills such as playing a musical instrument, learning a new sport, or any other type of mechanical skill. Although this drive is a natural one for those of us with A-type personalities, it is an impediment to those aiming for perfection and should be avoided at all costs.

Solid fundamentals are required to become the best in any skill, especially in firearms training. The problem comes from shooters having weak fundamentals and a desire for useless (and at times dangerous) or flashy techniques. Many times this is supported by firearms instructors either afraid to insist on perfection before moving on, or worse, a lack of understanding of their importance. This will eventually lead to a lack of virtuosity and a delay in truly mastering the art of shooting. It's vital to understand, especially in firearms training, where mistakes can be fatal, the importance of hammering on the basics of shooting:

1. *Shooting Platform*

2. *Grip*

3. *Sight Refinement*

4. *Sight Picture*

5. *Breathing*

6. *Trigger Control*

7. *Follow-Through*

Obviously, these are the seven fundamentals of marksmanship, but they must be truly mastered before you attempt to move on to more "advanced" shooting skills. Like the foundation of a building, your fundamentals need to be solid or everything you add on top will eventually come crumbling down. Sure it looks cool to run around the range like Captain America, but if your shots are missing the target you'll walk away looking like an idiot.

Look at the masters of any sport and how they train and you'll see they spend the majority of their time on basic skills. Michael Jordan is a great example of this and, whether you like basketball or not, most people know the story of how he became a legend in his sport: practicing the fundamentals — layups, free throws, and dribbling for hours more than everyone else. Jordan once said, "The minute you get away from fundamentals — whether it's proper technique, work ethic or mental preparation — the bottom can fall out of your game, your schoolwork, your job, whatever you're doing." There are many more examples in professional sports, just look for their faces on ESPN. But they don't practice for highlight reels; highlight reels happen by performing the basics with uncommon perfection.

The first place I learned this way of thinking was through karate as a child. The key elements I learned of a good karate practitioner are: stance, balance, focus, execution of technique, and follow-through. Sounds a lot like shooting, right? They are both martial arts. Both the shooter and karateka are warriors striving for perfection. A dedicated shooter will practice dry fire for hours, while the karateka does kata.

When I talk about perfection and mastery in combat shooting, I'm not talking about key-holing shots ... unless that's your goal. I'm talking about breaking down each fundamental and practicing it until it's perfect. (Hint: You'll never reach perfection ... so keep training!) What you do with these skills is totally dependent on the situation you're in or your course of fire. Virtuosity means something different to an IPSC shooter than it does to a Tier-1 shooter downrange or to the average guy who shoots a few weekends a month. Look at what you're training for and never settle for "good enough."

There are a wide variety of firearms instructors out there; some are good and some ... not so much. The quality I've seen ranges from great shooters that I continue to learn from to others who I wouldn't feel safe shooting next to on the same range. I don't want you to think I'm saying I'm the best or anyone else is the worst. I just want you to make an informed decision any time you're seeking instruction. Think about how they are as an instructor, not just as a shooter.

If I played football I'd want Vince Lombardi as my coach, not Aaron Rodgers. Just because Rodgers can pass well doesn't automatically mean he can teach you how to do it and vice versa for the greatest coach of all time. Just make sure you find out about an instructor's method of instruction: Do they insist on perfection of your fundamentals or do they insist on showing you cool-looking techniques? If you're training just so you can shoot cool videos to post on YouTube, that's one thing, but if you want to be a true master of your weapon and not just some guy doing a dance with a gun in your hands, then take a step back and check your fundamentals.

What will eventually cause the downfall of any training program is a trainer's lack of commitment to the fundamentals or the students' lack of insisting on its instruction. Rarely are instructors critical of minor details of the mechanics of shooting, which will eventually cause beginners to try and jump forward to the more advanced shooting techniques. In the end, this will lead to a shooter who looks cool but never seems to get any better.

As an instructor, it's natural to want to show my students fancy movements and advanced shooting techniques, but in the long run, I'm doing them a disservice. They've paid a lot of money and I want to show them how good I am, but my goal is to make them good shooters. I can't do that when I move away from the basics too quickly and onto the advanced material. Training is about making my students better shooters, not me.

In firearms training, you really need to nitpick the fundamentals of marksmanship and insist on them relentlessly with every shot you take. If you do this, you will be impressed by your progress and your mastery of the art of shooting. The sooner you learn that mastery of the fundamentals is the key to effective combat shooting, the sooner you will become a truly great shooter. By just committing to the basics of firearms training, your shooting will improve, you'll progress quickly, and you will gather an immense amount of respect from those around you. Seeing someone shoot with virtuosity is awe-inspiring to watch, and it's even better when you reach this level in your own shooting!

Throughout this book I'll be talking about certain habits you need to perfect to be a great shooter. The more time you spend practicing, the better you will become. If you're new to firearms and just want to know the basics of shooting, you can read through the book and you'll be better prepared for an occasional trip to the range. You don't need to set up a training schedule to get where you want to be, and that's fine. For others, you'll want to break down each technique and try each one out when you dry fire or go to the range. If you like a technique and find it's helping your shooting, then add it to your training regime and work on it becoming a habit when you shoot. We all have habits every time we shoot, some good, some bad. Becoming a better shooter is learning what habits are working and what ones aren't, and then replacing the bad ones and practicing them until you no longer think about them, until they are — habits.

"Excellence is an art won by training and habituation. We do not act rightly because we have virtue or excellence, but we rather have those because we have acted rightly. We are what we repeatedly do. Excellence, then, is not an act but a habit." ~ **Aristotle**

Safety

As a Navy SEAL, I've become very comfortable around firearms. But one of the things that make my fellow frogmen and me so comfortable around weapons is that we are very vigilant about adhering to the basic rules for firearms safety and handling. Anytime you forget about them, even for a second, bad things can happen ... and frequently do.

One day on the range I was teaching a basic pistol course to some new federal agents. The way this particular training was being run, there were other instructors from the unit we were training also on the line coaching the students. The line had been called cold; all weapons were cleared and checked by other students. I was on the other end of the line working with some students when the other instructor from the unit brought a group together to do a little "private" demonstration on trigger control. He brought his weapon up and slowly pressed back on the trigger ... as I'm sure you've guessed by now, the next thing that was heard was an ear-splitting, "**BANG!**" It seems this instructor (can I stop using that term for him now?) didn't think he needed to follow the same rules as the students, hell, the same rules as everyone else who handles weapons! In a word, he got cocky. Hi-speed, low-drag doesn't mean a thing to me if you don't know the condition of your weapon before you decide it's time to send that firing pin forward! Over the years I've seen it happen to other people on the range too and it makes me nervous. So I'd just like to make this clear: No one is so good with weapons that basic firearm and range safety rules don't apply.

The following is a list of safety rules that apply to any weapon, anywhere in the world. Some people make the mistake of calling these range safety rules, but it doesn't matter where you are, the four rules below always apply. Every range will also have a list of rules that apply to shooting at their facility (range rules), so make sure you follow those too. As with my story above, never assume that safety doesn't apply to you or that you're "better than that."

To Shoot Like a Navy S.E.A.L. your shooting needs to be:

Safe: Our colors are Blue and Gold, not Blue-on-Blue.

Effective: Our actions produce the desired result.

Adaptable: Every shooting situation is different and your skills need to be adaptable to address the situation.

Learned: It's not magic, it takes lots of practice and we also learn from the past.

Safety is more than just a rule — it's a tactic. If you're spending your time patching up a teammate from a blue-on-blue mishap, it's a lot harder to kill the bad guys. If it's good enough for the best warriors in the world, it's good enough for you!

Navy SEAL Firearms Safety Rules

1. Treat every gun as if it were loaded, regardless of perceived or actual condition.

I think this is the most important safety rule. If you treat all guns as if they are loaded, you really have to want to shoot someone for it to happen. Even if I know my gun is NOT loaded, before I give a demonstration, dry fire, or clean my weapon, I still check it again to make sure. Make sure you do the same and treat it like it's loaded until you've checked it by sight and touch. And never be embarrassed to ask for someone else to check your weapon to get confirmation.

2. Keep your finger off the trigger until ready to shoot.

Your finger should be indexed along the receiver until the decision to shoot has been made. It should also be removed from the trigger as soon as you no longer need to shoot, or your weapon is no longer pointed in a safe direction. Speaking of that ...

3. Always keep a gun pointed in a safe direction and never point your weapon at anything you do not intend to shoot.

Knowing where the muzzle of your gun is pointing at all times is critical to safely handling firearms. When we have problems with students during Close Quarters Combat (CQC) training, we sometimes attach a laser to their gun so they can better see where that gun is pointing and who would be taking rounds in the event of an accidental (AD) or negligent (ND) discharge. Even without a physical laser on your gun, you should imagine a laser coming out of your gun's muzzle and never let it cross the path of anyone else (unless of course you intend to shoot them).

4. Be sure of your target and know your target's foreground and background.

We hear it all the time on the range, "Who shot my target?" Not a big deal there, but what about when it's not training and lives are at stake? You need to be completely sure you know what you're shooting at, as well as what might be in front of it (walls, cars, barricades, trees) or what might move in front of it (cars, people, dogs) and what's beyond your target. This can be anything from people in the open to your family members in another room during a home invasion.

If your weapon has a safety, you'll need to remember one more: **Keep your weapon on safe until aimed in on target**. Four (or five) rules, it's not a long list and there are plenty

of other variations to use. Pick whichever verbiage you like and live them every day. Could you change the words from "intend to shoot" to "willing to destroy?" Sure, whatever you'll remember. They all mean the same thing and normally if you can even remember ONE of them, no one is going to die.

I recently began teaching my kids how to shoot, starting with a Daisy BB rifle and several Airsoft weapons. Before they could even touch the gun they needed to be able to not only regurgitate all four rules, but also explain what each one meant. Since the gun has a safety, they also needed to remember to keep the weapon "On safe until aimed on target." These guys were five and seven years old when they started; if they can remember them, I expect everyone else I shoot with to do the same.

Speaking of children and firearms, make sure they know the difference between real guns and "play" guns. My kids love their Nerf guns, but they know they are not real (although they still practice the same rules with them — remember it's "Don't point your weapon at anything you do not intend to shoot" ... I've been hit by a lot of Nerf darts!) When it comes to the real thing, avoid horseplay! Firearms are deadly and must be treated with the respect they deserve. They are not toys and should not be treated as if they were.

Always make sure a gun is empty before cleaning. It's impossible to verify if a gun is loaded just by looking at it.

Never presume or take another's word that it is empty — as President Regan would say, TRUST, BUT VERIFY! It only takes a second to check, and the time it takes could save a life.

Before you shoot, make sure the firearm is safe to operate. Guns need regular maintenance to remain operable. If you have any question concerning a gun's ability to function, a professional gunsmith should look at it.

Anytime you go to the range, make sure you know the range rules and wear eye and ear protection. Staying safe on the range is up to you. If you see someone doing something unsafe on the range, make sure you say something. So many times I see people point out unsafe actions on the range and not say anything. You not saying anything is as much of a safety violation as the person doing the act. Man-up (women can man-up too!) and tell them they need to stop. Remember, safety is everyone's responsibility.

Happy Shooting!

*My goal in writing this book series is
to cut through all that nonsense we have
seen or heard on the range and get to
what works.*

The Habit of Perfection

It's happened several times now. I show up at the range to work with a new group of shooters who are supposed to be "past the basics" of shooting. Operators who the government trusts to move around confined spaces with other people, carrying automatic weapons. As we start warming up, I'll go down the line and make corrections on stance, grip, trigger control, etc. and find out that they nod their heads in agreement, but when I ask them about the technique, they say they don't know what I'm talking about. I'm talking about the basics of shooting! The fundamentals of marksmanship that everyone with a gun in their hands needs to know to shoot well.

As a Navy SEAL these were ingrained in my head and repeated on a daily basis to achieve muscle memory. I know some people don't like this term. I've said it before during a class and someone wanting to make themselves sound scientific would say, "Technically your muscles don't have memories. You're actually training your neurons and...

blah, blah, blah." OK, thanks for the refresher on fifth grade biology. I'm just trying to make you a better shooter and communicating it in a way we can all understand. Don't muddy the waters with your technical nonsense.

My goal in writing this book series is to cut through all that nonsense we have seen or heard on the range and get to what works. If something I say in this book doesn't work for you, then don't use it! All I ask is that you give it a try. I've found cognitive dissonance to be the biggest limiting factor in helping experienced shooters to improve their skills.

Basically cognitive dissonance is when you've done something for a long time and even when presented with evidence that there is a better way, you subconsciously fight against it. To improve in any area, you need to first be open to change. There is a reason you came here looking for answers and I hope to provide some.

If you came here looking for confirmation that everything you've been doing is perfect, this might not be the book for you. As the saying goes, "There's more than one way to skin a cat." The techniques I present not only work, but they've been tested in combat. Of course there are other ways that work and if you're happy with where you're at as a shooter, then there is no reason to change. But if you're open to trying something new and possibly going against the way your NRA instructor taught you was "the right way" to shoot, then I'm sure you'll pick up enough golden nuggets of information for this read to be well worth your time.

As I stated earlier, shooting is all about habits, and the first habit you need is the habit of perfection. To be a good shooter, you need to be consistent. To be consistent, you need to have good habits. You need to do things the same way every time until they become ingrained in you and you do them without consciously thinking about it every time you fire your weapon. When you practice these techniques, never settle for "good enough" and always strive for perfection. Of course you'll never reach this goal, so it will force you to continue to train.

Being a good combat shooter is not magic and no one is born with the skills. If you want to be good, you need to train. If you want to be great, you need to train more. If you want to be the best, you need to train more than anyone else — you can see where I'm going with this. Not only do the skills you practice need to become habits, but also training itself must become a habit. It's not something you only do when you have time — you need to make time.

Reading this book will not make you a better shooter. Only training will make you a better shooter!

Combat Marksmanship Fundamentals

In this book I will cover the bedrock of firing any weapon system in combat. You'll learn it the way I learned as a Navy SEAL and the way I taught it as one of their leading instructors. These are the fundamentals of combat marksmanship that make good shooters on a range or competition, but are specifically designed for those on the battlefield. What's the difference between marksmanship and combat marksmanship? Quite a bit, really. Although they both require the same components (stance, grip, trigger control, etc.), the best way to accomplish these tasks vary depending whether you're fighting for your life, or just for the best score on a course of fire.

Don't get me wrong, I think shooting competitions are great and I don't pretend to have the skills the masters of that sport have. But make no mistake; combat is not a sport and the pressure you feel is a bit more than you get from a Pro-timer. So I'll be covering the seven Navy SEAL combat marksmanship fundamentals. Some may like to use three, five, or eight fundamentals; if it's easier for you to take a few of them and combine them in your mind, then do so. Just be warned: Leave one of them out when you're shooting and the round will miss its mark.

The SEAL Seven

1. Shooting Platform

2. Grip

3. Sight Refinement

4. Sight Picture

5. Breathing

6. Trigger Control

7. Follow-Through

In each chapter I will break down one of these seven combat fundamentals so they are not just a name or term you need to remember. You'll understand what they all mean, how to use them when you're shooting or dry-fire training, and why they're important in making you a better combat shooter.

As I began writing this book, I quickly wished I could show readers what I was talking about. You can only get so far with written descriptions, and even pictures normally only show you the starting and ending points. So by purchasing this book, you have access to exclusive instructional videos shot just for this book. I personally filmed these videos for you because if a picture is worth a thousand words, and if a video is shot at thirty pictures per second...that's a lot of words! You can access these free videos by going to http://howtoshootlikeanavyseal.com/videos.

The most important thing for you to do is to practice the techniques I describe in the book. I know that sounds simple, but sadly studies show that 75 percent of the people who actually finish reading this book will never utilize any of the techniques they've just learned. Some will finish this book, realize they're not magically a better shooter from reading it, and start looking for another book or video to make them a better shooter. There is only one way to get better at shooting and that is ... practicing! Once you have a basic understanding of the skills, any actual hands-on training you do will make you a better shooter compared to just reading another book or watching a video.

Shooting Platform

One of the biggest hurdles to being a good combat shooter is consistency, and this means doing things the same way every time you shoot. Specifically, what I'm talking about is your shooting platform or what some call body position or stance. Don't get me wrong, variety is the spice of life and this includes shooting. Try different positions, see what works and what doesn't, but when you find one you like, stick with it and work on consistency.

I'll be using the terms shooting platform, stance, and shooting positions interchangeably so don't get mixed up with their use. I try to use platform when I can, since for me the platform is something you work off of and can be moved, where as when I hear position I think of it being static. Since relatively few firefights are static, that's where I lean. But like I said, don't worry so much about their use for now since we need to get in a good position before we move anyway! Crawl – Walk – Run, right?

No matter what weapon system we're talking about or what position, a solid shooting platform is essential to good shooting. The more solid the position is, the easier it is to hold the gun and control the trigger without disturbing the sights. Whether you're shooting prone, kneeling, standing, or any unconventional shooting position, you should have as much of your body directly behind the weapon as possible. You need to be able to drive the gun, and just like driving your car you should have the seat (the platform you operate the car from) adjusted properly. Imagine trying to drive a car fast if you were sitting off to the left or right of the steering wheel. It would be hard to control it, right? Especially when you start moving! Well it's harder to control a gun if you're not behind it too.

Shooting positions should be flexible to allow modifications according to individual body structure. Just because I shoot well with my body positioned a certain way doesn't mean it will work the same for you. I'm 6'1" and someone 5'7" might not be able to contort their body the same way I do, so don't push it if it's not working. Think of my descriptions here as a starting point and just make sure you don't violate any of the fundamentals of a good shooting position. This flexibility becomes even more important on the two-way range as the shooter must assume the steadiest position that will also allow for observation of the target area and, if available, provide cover and concealment. Depending on terrain, vegetation, and the tactical situation, there are

innumerable possibilities. Remember, stay flexible and adapt to your surroundings. In combat, your feet are going to be where they need to be for mobility, cover, or concealment. Try to keep your weight forward and your center of gravity low and this will help keep your sights on target.

One of the things I teach my students is to have as many things pointing at the target as possible. This includes your head, eyes, toes, hips, shoulders, fingers, knuckles and thumbs. In a perfect world, on a flat range with no one shooting back at you, this is easy to do and should be practiced. But ultimately, control of the weapon needs to come from the upper body. Your lower body needs to be able to conform to the current tactical situation while the upper body drives the gun. If you're shooting and moving, think of your lower body like the tracks of a tank and your upper body as the turret. Your lower body is doing everything it can to give your upper body the best platform from which to shoot.

Three Elements of Any Good Shooting Platform

1. Bone Support

A good shooting platform employs bone support, not muscular support. A strong foundation is as necessary to shooting as it is to a well-built house. Think about this. You're using muscles to hold your weapon on target and you bring your focus back to the front sight and relax ... your body is going to move to its natural point of aim (see

below). You're not going to notice this subtle shift because you're not focusing on the target — you're focusing on the front sight, right?

2. Muscular Relaxation

Through training and the use of a natural point of aim, you need to learn to have muscular relaxation in all shooting positions. Undue strain or tension causes trembling, which is transmitted to the gun. When you're shooting in a standing position, see if you can wiggle your toes. It's the longest nerve in your body and if you're relaxed enough to wiggle your toes ... you're relaxed. In combat, you're going to have enough stress going on around you; your ability to relax enough to make accurate shots could just save your life.

3. Natural Point of Aim

Your natural point of aim is the place your sights are aiming when your body is relaxed. You're using bone support and have achieved muscular relaxation; when you look at your sights, that's your natural point of aim.

To find your natural point of aim in any shooting position do the following...

1. Take any shooting position and mount your weapon.

2. Once a sight picture is established, close your eyes, take a deep breath and exhale to your natural respiratory pause.

3. Concentrate on making your body completely relaxed. Doing this will cause the gun to fall to your natural point of aim.

4. If your gun is clear and safe, use this opportunity to dry fire once.

5. Open your eyes and adjust your position by shifting your lower body until the gun points to the target at the exact point where you want the bullet to strike. Do not make any adjustments using muscle; even very minor adjustments must be made with the lower body.

6. Go through steps 2–5 until when you open your eyes, your sights are exactly where you want them. That is your natural point of aim.

Go to http://HowToShootLikeANavySEAL.com/videos to register to receive your 12 free training videos.

Obviously in combat or most timed evolutions, you can't do this, but if you practice it enough your body will learn what a good shooting platform feels like and you'll naturally end up in a more advantageous position to deal with your threats. Even if you walk up to the firing line to do some training, take a moment to look at where your hips are pointing when you relax them. If they're pointing two target frames over, you may help yourself out by adjusting them to point at your target. The easiest way to do this is to simply turn your toes toward your target.

In all of the positions described here, the upper body (above the waist) is kept in the same position while the lower body (platform) is adjusted to allow firing from different heights or angles. As I mentioned earlier, all of these descriptions are just a starting point for you to use so you understand the fundamentals of a good stance. Normally, the only place you will ever be in a picture-perfect stance is on the range. In a gunfight you'll most likely be moving and adjusting your stance to fit your environment and the situation.

As always, use whichever stance works best for you. Whatever stance you choose, it should be athletic — something you can move into and out of quickly.

Pistol

Standing

Although there are several stances you can use for shooting the pistol, I'll be describing the stance I use, which is most closely labeled the modern or modified isosceles. This stance uses the geometric power of a triangle to support the gun. This shape allows for the use of bones, not muscle, to support the position. Think of how you would be standing if someone were going to tackle you. You'd be in a fighting position, right? Well, gun fighting is no different. You can see the strength of the position in the picture below. Notice how the arms form a perfect triangle.

The position is as follows:

1. Stand with feet shoulder-width apart (feet can be wider, if it feels better), toes pointed toward the target, knees slightly bent (5–10 degrees).

2. Drop the strong-side leg straight back until the toes are in line with the heel of the other foot. Again, you can slide this foot back farther to get into a more aggressive stance.

3. Both arms are fully extended and locked straight out but not over-extended. If you extend your shoulders out of the socket, you lose strength from your larger chest and back muscles. You should also not have any tension in the biceps when your arms are extended. You should shoot from wherever your arms naturally stop when extended. "Locked" does not mean tense.

4. The head is upright, leaning forward (nose over toes) at the waist.

5. Bring the sights up to the eyes.

6. Shoulders, arms, hands and gun will be in a straight line.

7. The barrel of the gun will be in line with the shooter's spine.

Go to http://HowToShootLikeANavySEAL.com/videos to register to receive your 12 free training videos.

Due to the locked joints and chest-forward aspect, there are several situations where this shooting platform may not be the best choice. For instance, if you are shooting out of a vehicle window or need to shoot while moving, a weaver-style stance with bent arms will likely work better. The key is to train for these situations and find out what works best for you.

Kneeling

As with standing, there are several common kneeling positions from which you can shoot effectively. The differences in the kneeling positions I'll describe all have to do with how low you go, either for stability, mobility or use of available cover. All these variances are done with the lower body only while the upper body will be in the same position as standing. The three positions I will cover are high, medium, and low kneeling. Some shooters like to shoot from a double kneeling position (both knees down), but I don't find this is a combat-effective position when I need to get up and go.

High Kneel

Drop straight down on strong knee from the standing position described above. Toes of strong-side foot are bent under to allow for quick movement and balance. The leg of the reaction-side leg is bent. Leaning forward at the waist, you should not be able to see your reaction-side foot. This position is the fastest to get into and out of while lowering the shooter's profile.

Medium Kneel

Drop straight down on strong knee from the standing position. Toes of strong foot are bent under to allow for quick movement. The leg of the reaction-side leg is bent. Sit back on the heel of the strong-side foot while leaning forward at the waist. This position is used to lower your profile from that of a high kneel and for increased accuracy.

Low Kneel

Drop straight down on strong knee from the standing position. The foot of the strong-side leg is bent under. Sit back on the foot. The reaction-side leg is bent while leaning forward quite a bit. This position is the slowest to get into and out of, has decreased stability, and is used to shoot under very low cover.

Go to http://HowToShootLikeANavySEAL.com/videos to register to receive your 12 free training videos.

Prone

The prone (face down) position is good to know should you find yourself on the ground during a gunfight. It's the most accurate position to shoot from when done properly and gets the shooter as low as possible. It's also the slowest to get into and out of and limits your field of view, but if practiced enough it can be worth your travel time.

To shoot from the prone position:

1. Lie face down on the ground with your legs spread apart, heels down. Your toes can be pointed in or out, just do not have your heels sticking up. The reason is that any movement in your heels will translate to the gun and increase your chance of error.

2. The upper body position is the same as standing and kneeling.

3. If possible, keep forearms and sides of hands on the ground for support and bring the head down to the sights.

4. If unable to get low enough to see the sights, rotate onto the strong-side arm just enough to be able to see the sights. The arms and gun position do not change; the entire upper body is rotated as a unit until the sights are on target. Make sure the reaction-side leg is in front of the strong-side leg. It can be bent or kept straight.

Go to http://HowToShootLikeANavySEAL.com/videos to register to receive your 12 free training videos.

Carbine

In classical marksmanship, there are four main shooting positions: prone, seated, kneeling and standing, which is sometimes called off-hand. These positions start off with the most stable (prone) and move up to the least stable (standing). As we are discussing combat marksmanship here, it must also be noted that they move from the least mobile (prone) to the most mobile (standing). Since the seated position is rarely used in combat, I'll only be describing the other three.

Again, these positions should be modified according to your body type and shooting style. There are also many other useful positions from which to shoot including shooting from the reaction side, shooting from retention, one-handed shooting (yes, with a carbine), squatting, fetal prone, urban prone, supine, etc. The important thing is to understand the fundamentals of a good position and make sure you are utilizing them in whatever position you find yourself.

One of the most important aspects of fighting with more than one weapon system is utilizing the same fighting position. You don't want to have to transition from your rifle to your pistol and also need to move your lower body, head, or chest. If you're in a good fighting position, you should be able to transition with no movement except from the shoulders down to the hands. As you read through these positions, note the similarities to the pistol.

Standing

This position is probably the most common you will find yourself using in any combat situation. It's the quickest to assume and allows for the most mobility — something you need to avoid getting shot.

To shoot from the standing position:

1. Stand with feet shoulder-width apart (feet can be wider, if it feels better), toes pointed toward the target, knees slightly bent (5–10 degrees).

2. Drop the strong-side leg straight back until the toes are in line with the heel of the other foot. As with the pistol, you can slide this foot back farther to get into a more aggressive stance.

3. Mount the weapon so the buttstock is in the shoulder (not hanging over the top) and directly below the strong-side eye. If this is not possible due to body armor, get it as close to the center of the chest as possible. Rather than thinking the buttstock should be placed into the shoulder, think of it needing to be placed in the chest. This more centerline placement helps with recoil management.

4. The head is upright, leaning forward (nose over toes) at the waist.

5. Bring the sights up to the eyes.

6. Shoulders, arms, hands, and gun will be in a straight, level line.

7. The strong-side hand (fire control) should grip the pistol grip on your carbine the same as you grip it on a pistol — high up with the wrist straight behind. Keep this elbow close to the body and pull the buttstock into your chest.

8. The reaction-side hand should grip the hand guard/ rail system as far forward as safely possible. I do not recommend using a vertical fore-grip to hold onto the

weapon. I think they are possibly the single worst things to ever happen to marksmanship.

9. Make sure some part of your hand (fingers or thumb) is above the barrel/on top of the gun to manage recoil.

10. Take away the hinge in your reaction-side elbow by rotating the elbow up and out.

11. Drive the gun with your reaction hand and leave your strong hand to operate the fire control system.

> Go to http://HowToShootLikeANavySEAL.com/videos to register to receive your 12 free training videos.

Kneeling

There are two kneeling positions I'll cover: unsupported and supported. Kneeling positions are used to utilize cover or lower your profile and keep you somewhat mobile. Many shooters will need to slide their reaction-side hand back closer to the magazine to find a comfortable position if getting into the supported position.

Unsupported

Drop straight down on strong knee from the standing position described above. Toes of strong-side foot are bent under to allow for quick movement and balance. The leg of the reaction-side leg is bent. Leaning forward at the waist, you should not be able to see your reaction-side foot. This position is the fastest to get into and out of while lowering the shooter's profile.

Supported

Drop straight down onto the strong knee from the standing position. Toes of strong foot are bent under to allow for quick movement. The leg of the reaction-side leg is bent. Sit back on the heel of the strong-side foot while leaning forward at the waist. Rest the triceps of the reaction-side arm onto the knee of the reaction-side leg. If this does not work for you, you may put your elbow on top of your thigh. Either way, make sure you have hard on soft (elbow bone to thigh muscle) or soft on hard (triceps to kneecap). This position is used to lower your profile from that of an unsupported kneel and for increased accuracy.

Go to http://HowToShootLikeANavySEAL.com/videos to register to receive your 12 free training videos.

Prone

This position is the most stable of all the positions covered and is used for the lowest possible profile and/or the greatest amount of stability. The flipside of this is that it's the least mobile of the fighting positions and it reduces your fields of fire both vertically and horizontally.

To shoot from the prone position:

1. Lie face down on the ground with your legs spread wide apart, heels down (get big). Your toes can be pointed in or out, just do not have your heels sticking up. The reason is that any movement in your heels will translate to the gun and increase your chance of error.

2. The upper body position is essentially the same as standing or kneeling.

3. Both elbows will be on the ground and used as outriggers for support.

4. Your body needs to be directly behind your gun, not off to the side like a little green army man. The barrel should be inline with your strong-side butt-cheek.

5. The support hand should be pulling the gun into your shoulder and you should be able to let go with your strong hand without the weapon moving.

6. The magazine should be used as a support if possible. Before relying on this in combat, make sure your gun will not jam if the magazine is used as a monopod. Test each type of magazine you have with your gun during training. If it passes the test, this is a very stable position.

Go to http://HowToShootLikeANavySEAL.com/videos to register to receive your 12 free training videos.

Obviously there are other positions, and even these are going to be drastically modified depending on the terrain where your firefight takes place. The point is to use these examples as what to strive for and a good starting point to practice. It's also important to note that everyone's body is different. We all have different levels of flexibility, our body parts are all different lengths, and hinge at different points. Like I said, use these as a starting point and modify to what fits your body; just remember the elements that make up a good shooting platform and try not to break any of the basic rules.

If you remember the basic elements of a good shooting platform and put them into practice on the range and in your dry-fire training, you'll be able to apply them no matter what position your body ends up in when it's time to deliver effective customer service to someone who asks for it.

Grip

No matter what weapon system you're shooting, a solid grip is vital to placing accurate rounds on target. As sure as having a loose scope mounted on a rifle will make it impossible to hold a group, a loose grip will cause rounds to fly aimlessly off their mark and leave you searching for impacts as well as answers. So in the same way you need to check your weapon before you shoot to ensure everything is tight, you need to check your grip to make sure you've got the best connection between yourself and the weapon.

Although many shooters focus on the trigger finger as the key to accurate shooting, I feel the grip holds the title as king of consistency. Think of it this way: If your grip is like a gun vise and there is no way the weapon will move, you can do whatever you want to the trigger! Now let's say that you've practiced pulling the trigger straight back until it's literally impossible for you to pull off to one side or the other even a fraction of a millimeter, but ... your grip sucks and the weapon moves inconsistently every time you squeeze the trigger (perfectly). Your shots will be all over the place! Maybe once in a while you'll get lucky and the recoil will be straight back (even broken clocks are right twice a day), but people calling you "Shotgun" will be the only constant on your range.

Grip holds the title as king of consistency.

Don't let the tail (your finger) wag the dog (your gun). Your contact with 99 percent of the gun is much more important than where you contact the remaining 1 percent of the gun. The reason most people focus on the wrong thing is that they start off with a poor grip and rather than fix that, think of ways to work around it. Let's start you off on the right path with a good grip.

Pistol

Guns are built to a variety of specifications and so are your hands, so it's a good idea to start off with something that fits your hand rather than try to adjust your grip to fit a gun. I recognize if you're in the military or law enforcement you probably don't get to pick the guns you use, so the techniques in this chapter will be particularly important to you. If you do get to pick your gun, make sure you head out to your favorite Gun Mart before you purchase online to see how it feels in your hand. Some guns these days have different grips or back-straps you can change out for a better fit, so check to see if these are available. The gun should fit comfortably in your hand with the forearm of your firing hand in a direct line behind the pistol. Your trigger finger should be able to reach the trigger without dragging along the side of the gun. We've all heard the saying, "If the glove doesn't fit, you must acquit." When it comes to guns, "If the gun doesn't fit, you're not going to hit."

Now that you've selected the right piece of equipment, let's talk about how to control that explosion going off in your hands. When you grip the gun, make sure that the forearm of your strong hand is in line with the barrel of the pistol. Just like I talked about in the first chapter, it's important to have as much of your body behind the gun as possible to control recoil, and it starts here with a pistol. Your hand needs to be as high up the gun as possible. In a perfect world you would

have your hand directly behind the barrel, but guns have moving parts up there making this impossible. Keeping this goal in mind, your hand should be high enough on the grip so the webbing of your hand is compressed on the beaver-tail. If your grip is too low it will not only affect your shots, but can also cause your weapon to jam from not having a solid recoil abutment.

Wrap your hand around the gun and make sure your trigger finger is not riding along the side of the grip as this can pull the gun off target when you press back on the trigger. Don't get caught up on placing your trigger finger in a certain spot on the trigger. Everyone's hands are built differently and what works well for a paper shooter on a one-way range may not work for you when you hear the snap of rounds whizzing past your pineapple. Just make sure you're able to press the trigger straight back while keeping your sights on target.

If you're using a two-handed technique (and I suggest you do whenever possible), the support (a.k.a. reaction) hand should be placed with the palm of the hand filling the space on the grip left by the strong hand. To do this, your support hand should be angled down at about a 45-degree angle. Make sure there is no space between the palms of your hands. Pressure should be equal in both hands as they torque toward each other like a vise. Some people teach a 60/40 grip for how hard you should be gripping the gun, but I prefer a 100/100 grip since that's what you're going to do

in combat and it's best to think about how you're going to drop the threat rather than how hard you're squeezing the gun with each hand. Both of your thumbs should be pointing forward, toward your target. I've found that the more things you have pointed at your target, the better chance you have at hitting it.

A lot of people have questions about how strongly they should grip a pistol, and I've found that consistency of grip equals consistency of shots. To be consistent without a pressure gauge there are only two options. One is to hold it with no power, just enough so it doesn't drop out of your hand. The other is with 100 percent power. Which one do you think will produce more consistent shots? How do you think you will be holding your weapon when you're being shot at? Also, the 100 percent grip cures "milking" the trigger. Try this: relax your hand and pretend to rapidly pull the trigger of a pistol with a heavy trigger pull. See your other fingers moving? This is "milking" the trigger. Now do it with your hard tightly clenched ... it's impossible to milk the trigger.

Now that you've got the perfect grip, put the gun back in the holster and take the time to note the position of your hand. You need to establish the proper grip in the holster and you need to practice getting the right grip every time. Did I hear someone say dry fire? Practice drawing the gun from its holster and bringing it up on target, making sure you have the right grip. Once you've got the gun in your hand and pointed at your target, the grip you've got is the one you're going to shoot with ... get it right.

Here are a few ways you can check for a proper grip:

- Let go with the bottoms of both hands and the gun should hang straight down.

- Point the gun straight up in front of your face. The trigger finger should be straight across from the reaction hand thumb.

- You should be able to support a pistol only with your reaction hand.

- You don't need to adjust your grip between shots.

- Your sights come back in the same way after recoil.

- You're shooting consistent groups.

Go to http://HowToShootLikeANavySEAL.com/videos to register to receive your 12 free training videos.

Carbine

The grip for the firing hand of a carbine is basically the same as on a pistol. Grip the rifle with your firing hand as high as possible with your middle finger touching the bottom of the trigger guard. This will help when doing magazine changes and clearing malfunctions. The gun is controlled with the support hand, leaving the strong hand to concentrate on fire control and pulling the buttstock into your shoulder. Before I talk about the forward grip of the carbine, I need to talk about accessories such as lights or lasers. Before you start tricking out your bang-stick with cool-guy gear, make sure you can shoot it accurately. Take it out to the range and establish a solid shooting platform and note where your forward hand grips the gun. Now look at the open space you have available ... this is where you need to mount any accessories. I see a lot of guys on the range saying they can't grip the gun properly because something is in the way. Don't let the tail wag the dog! You need to be able to shoot effectively first or that cool new light is only going to help your teammates find your corpse.

So now that we've cleared the playing field, grip your gun as far out on the handguard/rail as possible. I always ask my students, "If you were going to nail a 2x4 to a wall and only had two nails, where would you put the nails to give you the most support?" The answer is always the same, as far apart as possible. If you want to support your gun, you need to do the same thing.

There are a number of different ways to grip the handguard, but it's important that some part of your hand is above the level of the barrel. The recoil of the gun is going to kick the gun up. If you're trying to hold the gun from underneath it's going to bounce up and pull out of your hand every time. For the same reason, it's important that you take that hinge-point (elbow) out of the equation. Most people I see on the range shoot with the support elbow directly beneath the gun giving the weapon a perfect hinge to move around. This may be fine for slow-fire on a static range hitting bull's-eyes, but it is not going to cut it in combat. By simply rotating the arm out to the side, you eliminate the hinge and are better able to drive the gun with the reaction hand and send accurate rounds downrange as fast as needed. As with the pistol, I like to point anything I can at the target. In this case, depending on your grip, you can either point your thumb or your index finger.

Here are a few ways you can check for a proper grip:

- Let go with the strong hand. The gun should stay in your shoulder.

- Let go with the reaction hand. The gun should stay in your shoulder.

- When shooting, your sights come back in the same way after they recoil.

- You're shooting consistent groups.

Go to http://HowToShootLikeANavySEAL.com/videos to register to receive your 12 free training videos.

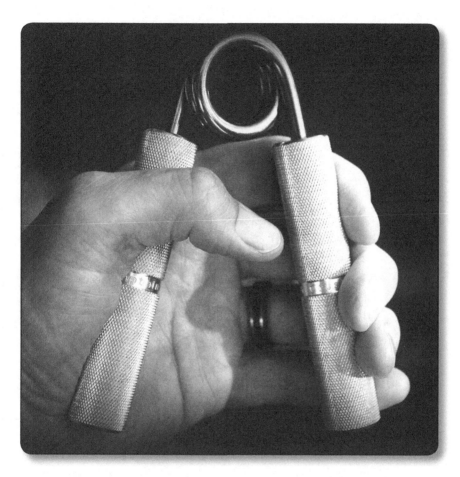

Here's a final piece of advice for a good grip, especially with the pistol. This one trick could cure 95.3 percent (made-up statistic) of all grip issues and I'm amazed by how few people do it ... Practice grip strength! I practice three times per week (Monday, Wednesday, and Friday) for about 10–15 minutes, normally on my way to a training site. I use Captain of Crush grippers, which are expensive compared to others, but they get results. If you've got a weak grip, your shooting is likely to be the same.

Sight Refinement

I'm always surprised by how many shooters out there have never learned the basic fundamentals of marksmanship. Then there are others who learned the fundamentals and have been slinging lead for years, but may have neglected to practice the skills needed to put effective firepower downrange using those little pieces of metal protruding from the tops of their guns. So here I will be discussing how to properly align (and refine) your sights in the event your scope, red-dot, or laser ends up quitting the fight before the enemy does.

Right after the invention of rifling, I put sight alignment as the second most important contribution to man being able to fire an accurate shot. Sight alignment and sight picture are two terms that are often used interchangeably and many times used as one and the same. It's fine to put them together once they are both understood, but it is vital to know that they are two different and very distinct components. Sight alignment has nothing to do with the target (well, besides hitting it), while sight picture has little to do with your sights.

In order for you to provide exceptional customer service, you must aim the gun and give the round a definite direction of travel to the target. Accurate aiming with open sights is achieved by placing the front sight exactly in the middle of the rear sight with the top of the front and rear sight posts flush and equal amounts of light on either side of the front sight post. (fig. 1) With an aperture or peep sight, this is accomplished by putting the tip of the front sight post centered vertically, as well as horizontally, in the rear sight aperture. It then becomes imperative that the shooter maintains this relationship between the front and rear sights while depressing the trigger and discharging the weapon.

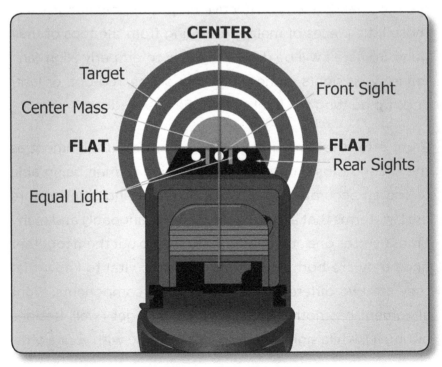

fig 1 Proper sight alignment

Sight alignment has to be worked out with each type of gun you shoot, but the basics remain the same. There are a lot of different types of sights out there and it's important to know how the manufacturer intended yours to be used. Some owner's manuals will even include pictures or descriptions on how they should be aligned. If you're like me, you don't read directions, but maybe you could take a peek when no one is looking ... it could save you a lot of time and headaches on the range.

As you are first learning to align your sights, there are a few things that can go awry, but if you're armed with the right knowledge, you'll be better prepared to make self-corrections. The first is known as an Angular Shift Error. (fig. 2) This occurs if you fail to correctly align the sights as described above. As the amount of the error or the distance from your target increases, the hope for hitting the target decreases exponentially, except in rare cases where a round is accidently "thrown" into the target. If you're not aligning the sights with the same military precision required of a Marine Corps recruit folding his underwear, each time you shoot the front sight post will be in a slightly different relationship with the rear sight and it will look more like you're shooting buckshot than a finely tuned instrument of destruction.

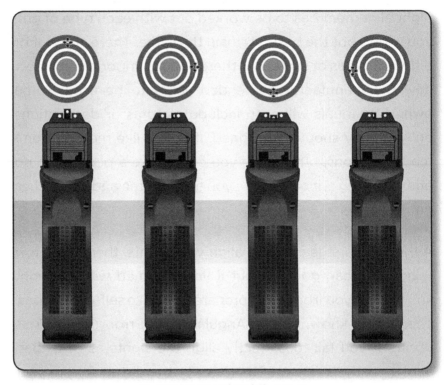

fig 2 Four angular shift errors

The other problem, which has more to do with sight picture than sight alignment, is called a Parallel Shift Error. This happens when the sights are aligned perfectly but the gun is not aligned perfectly with the target. Basically what this means is that if you're shooting at an eight-inch target, you can move your gun around in an eight-inch circle, no matter how far away you are, and you'll still hit the target in the same place your gun was in your imaginary circle back on the firing line. (fig. 6) If you're focused on the target instead of the front sight, small movements (the notorious wobble) will appear magnified. This movement, though still there, will appear significantly reduced by focusing on your front sight. The take away for all this gun-fighting geometry is that a bad sight alignment (angular shift error) is far more detrimental than sight picture (parallel shift error within the target size) to hitting your target. (fig. 3) The majority of the shooter's efforts should therefore be toward keeping the sights in correct alignment. So don't worry about your wobble ... holding the gun perfectly still is neither required, nor is it possible without support.

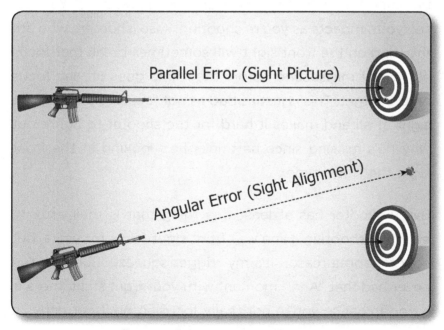

fig 3 Parallel vs. angular shift errors

Now comes the really tough part, Front Sight Focus! If you've been around guns for any length of time, I'm sure you've heard it, but what does it mean ... and more importantly, can you do it? What this means is that the front sight should be crystal clear, with the rear sights and target appearing blurry. I get it; this goes against everything your mind is screaming at you ... to focus on the target! But you need to fight that internal battle and focus only on the front sight. (I'll discuss this when your mind is right later in the chapter.) You also need to keep your eye on the front sight throughout each shot (which will also be covered later in the book) and not look at the target between each shot. You know you might be doing this if: (1) Your shots are going low, or (2) You can see your impacts as you're shooting! Also, shooters who are focusing on the front sight will sometimes break that focus at the last millisecond before the round goes off and focus on the target. This is just as bad as not focusing on the front sight at all and makes it hard for the shooter to figure out why he's missing since he thinks he's looking at the front sight the whole time.

Every shooter has at least one thing that is their crux to effective shooting. Mine was front sight focus for years, but now for some reason it's my trigger squeeze. But if you've never had that "Aha!" moment with your front sight, there is a good chance you're not really focusing on it correctly. In every course I run with new group, even with experienced shooters, there is always at least one shooter who is not focusing on his front sights. I'll have them bring the gun up, focus on the sight, and then describe to me in minute detail, exactly what the sight looks like as they are pressing back on the trigger. When the gun goes off, they see that by some miracle the bullet-fairy delivered the round to its intended target ... Aha! If you haven't had that moment, next time you're at the range, just point your gun at a target, focus on the front sight and say, "OK, I know it's not going to work, but I'm going to keep focusing on the front sight until the gun goes off. I follow through, and my gun is back on target." I think you'll be pleasantly surprised.

It is crucial to maintain front sight focus throughout the entire shot, but especially from when the round goes off until you get your next sight picture. Many times you will hear people say you should concentrate on the front sight, but I think this term is wrong. The definition I found for concentration is to, "direct toward one point." If you're concentrating on one point, that means you're not thinking about anything else and there are far too many other things vital to shooting to be neglected. In the same way as when you're driving your car through a tight space, you don't focus on one spot; you take in all the visual input and your eyes steer the car safely through the space. You're not thinking, "Red car on the right is 4 inches away, the blue car on the left is about ½ a foot away and ..." you're driving with your eyes. You must shoot the same way. Maybe it's just semantics, but I suggest you let your eyes focus on the front sight as your mind relaxes and takes in and processes all the data needed to deliver a well placed shot. With an open mind and the picture of what your eye needs to see in your mind, let your eyes pull the trigger and practice visual patience. If the shot is not there, you need to be patient and wait until it is. Too many shooters try to force a shot that's not there and waste a round or worse. I've heard it for many years and it's true — you can't miss fast enough to win a gunfight.

Col. Jeff Cooper wrote, "If there is one thing that is most vital about pistolcraft it is concentration on the front sight." Now I'm not arguing with the wisdom of the father of the modern technique of handgunning, I'm just contending his choice of the word "concentrate." I don't believe in the "Front Sight, Front Sight, Front Sight" mantra that I was taught (I was taught you're supposed to just say it in your head as you shoot). As a Master Training Specialist (MTS), I learned that people learn and perform much better from visual input than from auditory (this is why visualization works and people who talk to themselves are just crazy). So rather than saying the words "front sight," I recommend putting a picture of what the front sight should look like in your mind and not continue pressing back on the trigger unless that is what you see with your eyes.

By concentrating only on the front sight, you can lose awareness of sight alignment, break the shot, and throw a round ... you can't take it back. This is why I think he should've used the word "focus." By focusing, like with meditation, you are actually taking in all the information around you, not clearing your mind as is often thought. When you focus on the front sight, your eye will use your peripheral vision to keep your sights aligned.

Inattention to correct sight alignment can often be traced back to the failure to fully understand its importance (now you don't have that excuse). Without this knowledge you may very well start off on the right track, getting everything lined up just right, but then get front sight tunnel vision and lose correct sight alignment as you continue to press the trigger. Or if you start to notice a wobble, you'll lose focus on the front sight to make sure you're still on target and will then lose sight alignment (angular), which as we learned earlier is much more important than sight picture (parallel). No more excuses!

Now that you understand the importance of always focusing on your front sight ... I can tell you that there are definitely times when you will not want to (or need to) focus so keenly on your sights. Depending on the threat, distance, time available and possible collateral damage, you will need to decide where you will direct your focus during any engagement process. If you're close to your target and speed is more important than pinpoint accuracy, you will use a target priority focus (TPF). On the other hand, if you're farther away from your target, have more time or need to make a precision shot on a low percentage target, you'll need to use a sight priority focus (SPF).

When making this decision on where to focus, it's important to note that it's not an all-or-none decision. You're not just focusing on the sights or just focusing on the target; like exposure on a camera, it's a sliding scale of where your priority is and that scale will be constantly changing throughout the gun battle or competition. You could have someone pop up close to you with his gun drawn. You're only three yards away and he's facing you, standing up against a brick wall = Target Priority Focus – Engage. You then look up and see another threat twenty-five yards away. He is looking at your team waiting for a chance to take another shot at them. You can just see the side of his head and the angle you're at is not optimal since if you were to miss the threat, your round could sail past and hit a bystander = Sight Priority Focus – Engage. Check you out Hero!

Another way we like to miss shots is what I touched on earlier — lack of visual patience. You're waiting for the shot to break and it's taking longer than expected, so you just start slapping the trigger like it owes you money. In the process, you lose sight alignment ... and the round. Don't get anxious for the round to go off. Relax and let your mind process what's going on. If you've been told to just keep steady pressure on the trigger until the gun goes off, make sure you also keep your foot on the gas as your car spins out of control. Don't feel bad, I was taught the same thing, but treat your trigger like a gas pedal and if you're losing control, let off the gas! Once you're back in control, let your eyes control the trigger as you keep the sights aligned until the shot breaks. Remember, you can only shoot as fast as you can see. You need to wait as long as it takes to see what you need to see before you shoot. The only other option is missing the shot. You'll then need to make up the shot (if possible) and hopefully you didn't hit something you were not willing to destroy. As the saying goes, Speed is fine — accuracy is final.

This is why I like to refer to sight refinement, rather than sight alignment. For me, to align something is a one-time deal — line up the sights and then go to the next step — pull trigger. But refinement is something that continues — you line up the sights and keep them aligned as you go to the next step. Think in terms of sight refinement instead of sight alignment. It's not a one-time thing (align and shoot), it's a constant process that needs to be adjusted and managed until the follow-through. Missing one-hundredth of a second of visual input is enough to make you have no idea where your shot went. If this slight change of words helps you remember to keep adjusting (refining) your sight alignment as you press back on the trigger, then use it. If you've used the term sight alignment for 20+ years and you know you need to keep aligning them, then use that. I don't care what you use as long as it helps you put effective rounds downrange.

Since we're talking cars, is it better to drive with one eye open or two? I'm not a professional racecar driver, but I'm guessing the answer would be two. Two eyes are needed to locate threats quickly and it's physically impossible to close one eye without affecting the other at least slightly. I read one study that said vision is degraded in the opposite eye by as much as 20 percent and that the pupil will compensate for the closed eye by dilating. Normally this is a good thing as it lets in more light, but the amount of dilatation is not consistent with the lighting and this further deteriorates vision. So if rapid target acquisition and accurate shooting are on your "nice to have" list, then keep both eyes open. This becomes even more important if you are on a two-way range and you plan on moving at some point (highly recommended). I don't need a study to tell me that it's easier to walk (or run) with both eyes open.

A few people have vision issues that do not allow them to focus with both eyes open, but don't put yourself in that group too fast. It's going to be hard for anyone who's never done it before to learn, but the benefits are well worth the effort. You'll start out seeing double and it will probably be blurry, but there are some easy drills you can do to speed up the process of teaching your mind which picture (eye) to focus on. The first can be done at home or the office and all you need is a pen or pencil. Hold the end of your non-non-gun (pen or pencil) upright at arm's-length and place it over anything you designate as a target. First try to let your eyes figure out which one is right, then close your non-dominant eye and see if it's correct. If it is, great!

If not, with your non-dominant eye still shut, move it to your target and then open your non-dominant eye to teach your mind what it should focus on. Keep doing this until you start seeing one sight picture centered on the intended target. Of course this can be done with an unloaded weapon, just make sure you observe all safety rules that go along with this. The next thing you can do is to put a piece of clear tape or Vaseline on your shooting glasses over the non-dominant side. It only needs to be big enough to cover the part of your vision where the front sight post would be. Then shoot with both eyes open and this will help train your mind to associate the correct eye to the sight. I guess now is a good time to mention dry-fire training since all of this can be trained without having to go to the range or waste white pasties covering your misses. If after all this you still can't hit the broadside of a barn with both eyes open, then shut that other eye tightly and fire away! Better to make accurate shots than to miss and potentially hit an innocent bystander.

Finding Your Dominant Eye

You may be surprised to learn how many people shoot for years without ever knowing which eye is their dominant one. Approximately two-thirds of the population is right-eye dominant and one-third is left-eye dominant, but there are also a very small percentage of people who do not have a dominant eye. Sometimes people assume that since they are right-handed they are right-eye dominant.

This is the case about 90 percent of the time, but not always. Others are taught how to shoot by someone who is either right or left-eye dominant and just follow what they see. It's important to note that your dominant eye does not mean the eye with better vision; it's the eye that your brain says wins the coin toss in the minor differences between the two pictures each eye sends to your brain.

If you've never actually checked to see if you are left or right eye dominant, now is the time to do it. If you're new to shooting, this is where you need to start:

The Miles Test (Static)

1. Fully extend your arms in front of you.

2. Pick out a small object in front of you.

3. Make a triangle with your hands, with the object in the center of our triangle.

4. Keeping your hands in place, alternate closing each eye.

5. The eye you can still see the object with (when the other is shut) is your dominant eye.

The Miles Test (Moving)

1. Fully extend your arms in front of you.

2. Pick out a small object in front of you.

3. Make a triangle with your hands, with the object in the center of our triangle.

4. Keeping both eyes open, move your hands toward your eyes.

5. The eye you bring your hands to so you can still see the object is your dominant eye.

The Porta Test (Static)

1. Pick out a small object in front of you.

2. Fully extend your arm in front of you and point directly at the object.

3. Keeping your finger in place, alternate closing each eye.

4. The eye you are still pointing at the object with (when the other is shut) is your dominant eye.

The Porta Test (Moving)

1. Pick out a small object in front of you.

2. Fully extend your arm in front of you and point directly at the object.

3. Keeping both eyes open, move your finger toward your eyes while still pointing at the object.

4. The eye you bring your finger to is your dominant eye.

Go to http://HowToShootLikeANavySEAL.com/videos to register to receive your 12 free training videos.

Possible Outcomes:

Normal-Eye Dominant: You're right handed and right-eye dominant or you're left handed and left-eye dominant. You're on easy street!

Cross-Eye Dominant: You're right handed and left-eye dominant or you're left handed and right-eye dominant. The important thing is that you know ... you're a mutant! No seriously, you may need to turn (not tilt) your head left or right depending on which is your dominant eye to line up with the sights.

B-Eye Dominant: Like I said, not very common, but some people are both-eye dominant or neither-eye dominant. (Don't look up that name, because I just made it up.) You have a few choices. Some people will be dominant with different eyes at different distances. If this is you, then just be aware and use the correct eye. Some people will have a hard time focusing with either eye and may benefit from covering one of their shooting lenses with clear tape to blur one of their eyes. Finally, if this is a real problem, you can "treat" this and train one of your eyes to be dominant. You'll need to see an optometrist to learn how to do it correctly.

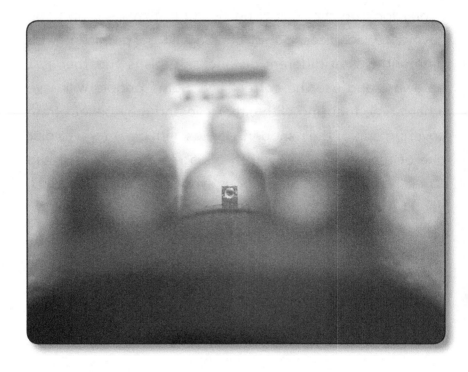

Sight Picture

Now that you understand that sight alignment is simply centering the front sight in the rear sight, we're going to talk about sight picture, which is taking that perfect sight alignment and aiming it at a target. As I discussed in the previous chapter, sight alignment is not as simple as point and shoot (or shouldn't be). There are a few things you need to keep in mind if you plan on walking away from a two-way range.

Here I'll be using the terms sight video and sight alignment interchangeably. What's the difference? In the same way that you can't just line up your sights and shoot (sight alignment), you also can't just take one picture of your threat(s) and call it a day. You need to constantly see what's changing. In combat, or even in some competitions, your targets move! The picture you took for your first round may not be effective for your second round. Even if your target is not moving, when the first round hits, your target could fall and you'll need to adjust your point of aim to fire for effect. But once again, if sight video works for you, use it. If it doesn't, but you still understand the importance of 'taking multiple pictures and combining them together in a way that conveys movement' ... well, you get my point.

Before we get started, I need to talk about some more old-school advice that many shooters, including myself, were taught and needs to be corrected. I'm talking about a center mass hold verses a six o'clock (a.k.a. lollipop or pumpkin-on-a-post) hold. I thought the six o'clock went away with the mullet, but I'll still find students on the range practicing this ancient technique. If you're using a six o'clock hold, I'm going to give you three scientific reasons why you need to change your evil ways to become a better shooter. If you're afraid of change, please skip this part. If not, continue on and feel free to impress your friends with this newfound knowledge.

The first reason is speed of accurate shot placement. If you are bringing your weapon up on target, you'll need to take extra time to figure out where you need to hold so your rounds land in the center of the intended target area. How about we skip this extra step and just aim center mass from the beginning? Rapid target acquisition is your friend when shooting, whether it's in a competition, on the battlefield or late at night when an intruder enters your home. Do you need to learn and practice mechanical hold-offs? Of course! But don't let it be your starting point.

The second reason is that your rounds will hit different places depending on the size of your target and your distance. I'm not sure why someone would practice different holds for different shaped targets, but some people have told me that the six o'clock hold is only used for bulls-eye type targets. Fair enough if all you're doing is shooting bulls-eye targets, but this book is about combat shooting. The problem would then become, how big the diameter of the circle is and at what distance you are shooting.

I sometimes exaggerate things to try and figure out if something will work or how it works. Let me give you an example (fig 4). Let's assume you shoot with a six o'clock hold. You go to the range after work to do some shooting, but the only target you have in the back of your car is one that's a 300-foot diameter bulls-eye ... and we'll say you're going to shoot from a distance of ten yards. (Like I said, I like to exaggerate!) After you load up and get that target set up with the help of a nearby crane, you step up to the firing line and try to decide which hold is better. For the first magazine you decide to use the center hold. The crane is still available so you get hoisted up to the center of the target, call the line hot and then unload the entire magazine in 3.4 seconds concentrating on sight alignment while merely pointing in the general vicinity of the center of the target. Not the best shooting you've ever done, but all shots are within twelve inches of the center of the target.

After you get lowered down, you reload and try out the 6 o'clock hold, the one you were taught in boot camp in 1922. You take your time because you're on solid ground now and fire the whole magazine really concentrating on the fundamentals of marksmanship. (You've got to shoot well to prove this is the best way!). Although you've got a tighter shot group (because you weren't up on a crane), the shots are a little low compared to the other group. You break out your tape measure and discover that there is a 149-foot, ten-inch difference in the two groups. To decide which one is closer to the center, you hop on your ATV and ride back about half a mile. From this vantage point you can see that the groups shot using the center hold are much closer to the center than the six o'clock hold group. (DAMN YOU!)

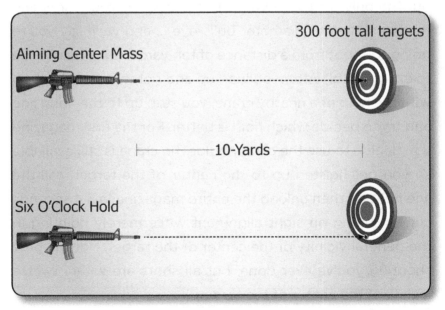

fig 4 Comparing holds on a 300-foot target at 10 yards

If you were wondering if the distance you shot from would have similar effects, they will. Hold center mass and leave the pumpkins on a post for Halloween.

The final reason I put away my six o'clock hold with my Walkman has to do with how your eye works. In the previous chapter I talked about the importance of front sight focus. I'm going to assume you read that (if not, do it now!) and that you're a good student and already practicing this important point. When you use the six o'clock hold and focus on the front sight, the target becomes blurry and this is where the problem lies (fig 5). The six o'clock hold might have a leg to stand on if the target were not blurry, but the target is blurry and therefore your eye can't find the exact bottom of

fig 5 Comparing holds on a blurry target

that pumpkin. Each time you shoot, your shots are going to move around as your eye tries to figure it out. The eye is an amazing thing and one of its traits is the ability to find the center of anything. This is why the center hold wins again. Although the target is blurry, it's still round and your eye can still find the center of it! This is true no matter what shape the target is and your eye can do it before you even think about pressing the trigger.

OK, so now back to our subject. Proper sight picture is when you take your sight and place it on (overlay) a target. The thing to remember is that sight picture only has to be on the target (anywhere on the target) to score a hit while sight alignment needs to be perfect or you risk missing the target completely. I guess that makes it hard for me to get you to continue reading this chapter now that I've downplayed its importance, but keep reading because, like I said in the beginning, there's more to it than just point and shoot...Really!

The reason sight alignment is more important than sight picture was explained in detail when I described the differences between angular and parallel shift errors. To recap, imagine that you're shooting at an eight-inch circle and that the circle is at the end of an eight-inch diameter tube. I'm sure they could set something like this up on Top SHOT, so it shouldn't be too hard to imagine. If it is, please see figure 6 below. If your sight alignment is right, you can fire anywhere into that tube as long as you're pointing somewhere at the target and

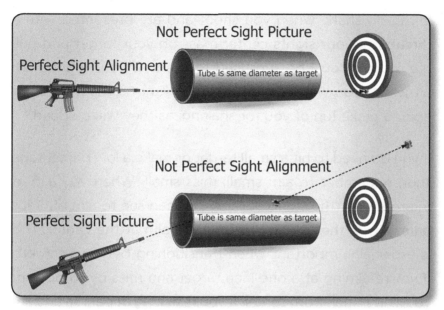

fig 6 Comparing sight alignment to sight picture

you'll hit the target. Whereas if your sight alignment is off, just a little, you're likely to miss the target completely, even if your front sight is pointed directly at the center of the target.

Many shooters don't understand this part of marksmanship and spend all their effort worried about a little wobble, rather than ensuring their sights are properly aligned. That little wobble will move you around the target, but how big is your wobble area? If you're shooting an eight-inch target, you've got eight inches to wobble! NOTE: If your wobble is eight inches or more, please clear and safe your weapon and go see your doctor. Unless you're trying to shoot gnats at twenty-five yards, don't worry so much about your wobble and concentrate on what's important.

If you do shake when you shoot and are presented with a threat, put your sights center mass on your target and pull the trigger. You'll be surprised to see that your rounds will hit where you were aiming and that your target will not be able to make fun of you for shaking, as they will be dead.

If you do need to hit a small target or make a low percentage shot, remember to aim small, miss small. When you aim at a target, pick the smallest thing you can see to aim at. If it's bare, divide the target into four and aim at the center. This is especially important when transitioning between targets. If you're aiming at a one-inch target and miss by 10 percent you'll hit 1.1 inch from center. If you're aiming at person and are 10 percent off, you could easily miss your target completely. Aim small, miss small!

All the things we do in marksmanship come down to having proper sight alignment and sight picture when the round goes off. Those are really the only things that matter in marksmanship.

Body Position: Is only important because it allows you to hold proper sight alignment.

Grip: You need to grip the gun correctly so you can maintain sight alignment.

Breathing: You breathe to relax with a handgun so you can focus on the sights, and you shoot during your natural respiratory pause with a rifle so your sight picture is the same with each shot. You continue to breathe in combat shooting so your eyes can continue to focus on your sight alignment.

Trigger control: The only reason you need to control the trigger is so you don't disturb the sights. If the gun was in a vise, you could slap that trigger till the cows came home and it wouldn't change where the round went.

Follow-through: Once again, this is just to preserve the sight alignment.

And the fundamentals of combat marksmanship are just the beginning. The only reason we need to have the same cheek-weld, eye relief, head tilt or anything else we do when firing a gun is all done in the quest to establish and maintain sight picture and sight alignment long enough to fire a shot without disrupting either one and quickly follow up with shots if needed.

Backup Sights/BUS

The only thing I call "backup sights" are the ones in my gun bag that I can put on in the event something traumatic happens to the sights on my gun. Iron sights need to be thought of as a tool in your toolbox. If you run a red dot on your long gun and you're shooting long distances (this distance can vary depending on the size of your red dot), the right tool for that job might not be your red dot. Maybe it's those things you've been calling "back-ups." It's the same reason you shouldn't call your non-shooting hand your "weak" hand, it's just doing something else, but still important. It's important that you learn how to shoot with your iron sights first before using optics anyway; it will make you a better marksman.

Sight picture with optics is more important than sight alignment because you get your sight alignment done when you sight in your gun. After you sight in, the only thing you need to worry about is your sight picture and this is made easier by the way optics are designed. What an optic does is to put the reticle (dot) on the same focal plane as the target so you just need to put it where you want to hit, and hold it there until the shot breaks. One thing I will point out is that red-dot optics should be mounted at arm's length on your rifle as they work best at that distance from your eyes. Doing this also helps you to have a wider field of view when acquiring targets and shooting. If it's too close to your eye, it will be like trying to assess the battlefield while looking through a toilet paper tube.

*"For breath is life, and if you breathe well
you will live long on earth."*
~Sanskrit Proverb

Breathing

OK, this one has always puzzled me. When I hear the term breathing, I assume it has something to do with oxygen being exchanged in the lungs via the pie-hole. But whenever I hear people talking about it as it relates to marksmanship, it always seems to be some form of holding your breath ... not breathing! So once again I'm here to right a wrong that has been perpetuated throughout our community for many years and get you on the road to recovery. Sit back, take a deep breath, and relax as I discuss proper breathing for combat marksmanship.

Years ago I remember being taught what many of you were also taught in regards to breathing as a marksmanship fundamental ... to hold your breath. At the time it made sense. I was being told this by an instructor who was a better shooter than me and who was running the course of instruction I was attending. I was in the military at the time and being taught by some of the best shooters in the world. Specifically I was told to, "Shoot during the Natural Respiratory Pause." I did this for many years as a SEAL Sniper and never found any reason to question what I had learned.

Now before my long-range brethren attack me, there are times that this technique should be used, and that is when taking long-range shots. What is long-range? That's a topic for a later discussion, but for now let's define it as any range that is nearing the max effective range of you or your weapon system. For these distances it is still important to use every fundamental to your advantage to ensure your round finds its intended target. But just as shooting during your natural respiratory pause helps in long-range shooting; it is extremely detrimental on a fast-paced battlefield.

From a scientific standpoint, your body needs energy to do work. For example, muscles need energy to contract, and all parts of your body need energy to synthesize necessary molecules. Your body gets the energy it needs by combining food molecules with oxygen in a process called cellular respiration. Your body combines sugar glucose with oxygen to release energy your body can use. The chemical reaction would look something like this:

$$C_6H_{12}O_6 + 6\ O_2 \rightarrow 6\ CO_2 + 6\ H_2O =$$
energy your body can use

Like your body, fire also needs fuel and oxygen to sustain itself. Your muscles and other parts of your body, like your eyes, need to have a constant supply of glucose and oxygen to provide energy for your muscles and to support other body functions. All parts of your body depend on breathing and circulation working together to deliver the oxygen needed by your body's cells and to remove the carbon dioxide produced by all cells in the body.

The Effects of Lack of Oxygen

The part of your body that is most sensitive to lack of oxygen is your brain. If there is a lack of oxygen, your brain is immediately affected, and if this continues, parts of the brain can be permanently damaged. The next body parts that are affected by lack of oxygen are your eyes, and both of these systems are critical to combat shooters.

The following is a list of effects on the body from a lack of oxygen.

This list was produced by The National Institute of Neurological Disorders and Stroke:

Motor Skills

The cerebellum is responsible for much of our coordinated movement and balance. Cell death can lead to jerkiness and other motor problems. An onset of poor coordination can be a sign of oxygen deficiency in the brain. With oxygen levels low, brainpower becomes focused on preserving core life functions over fine motor skills.

Visual Acuity

After the brain, the next body part affected from lack of oxygen is the eye. Although the first effects may be minor and hard to notice, your eyes' ability to focus is immediately diminished as the level of oxygen supplied to the eye

"When the breath wanders the mind also is unsteady. But when the breath is calmed the mind too will be still, and the yogi achieves long life. Therefore, one should learn to control the breath."
~ Svatmarama, Hatha Yoga Pradipika

decreases. If oxygen is withheld longer, the eye can develop a nystagmus, which is an involuntary movement.

Heart Rate

When the brain is not receiving enough oxygen, the heart rate will increase in an attempt to deliver more oxygen.

Concentration

With mild oxygen deficiency to the brain, you will notice difficulty with concentration and attentiveness. This difficulty with mental tasks can extend to poor judgment.

We all know that breathing is an essential part of life, but it is also an essential part of shooting. Look again at the list above and you'll find lack of fine motor skills, eye movement, jerkiness, increased heart rate, difficulty concentrating, and poor judgment ... not things you want to have in the middle of a firefight! Because of the misunderstanding many shooters have with this marksmanship fundamental, most shooters I work with are holding their breath as they try in vain to hit their targets. As they hold their breath, their vision quickly deteriorates and their hands begin to tremble. As their shot groups widen, they revert to what they were previously taught and try to hold their breath even more, making the situation worse. Effective shooting is all about relaxing and you can't relax while holding your breath. Your eyes' ability to focus on the front sight is also hampered while holding your breath, so it's important to give your body the oxygen it needs.

So we know we don't want to hold our breath when we shoot, but we do need to control our breath. If you have been exerting yourself and are huffing and puffing like a three-pack-a-day smoker on a 5k run, then you need to slow your breathing down to control your sights. The best way I've found to accomplish this is through a technique called autogenic breathing. This is simply taking a deep breath for a count of four, holding for a count of four and then exhaling for a count of four. Repeat this three times and it should help to slow down your breathing enough to control your sights. You can do this as you're getting ready to shoot or even while you're shooting.

For effective combat shooting, you should do your best to breathe normally. Relax and breathe throughout your trigger pull and you'll find it much easier to acquire and maintain a good sight picture.

Try breathing the next time you're dry firing or are at the range. Not only is it good for your body, but it's good for your shooting as well! If you're taking that long-range shot, go ahead and shoot during your natural respiratory pause, but if not give your brain and your eyes the oxygen they need to let them do their jobs.

Trigger Control

Trigger control. It's all about touch, and what I'm about to tell you is a touchy subject to many. So before I get started, I want to talk a little more about cognitive dissonance in training. Cognitive dissonance is the feeling of anxiety when you are presented with conflicting ideas. When it comes to firearms training, this would be when you've learned and practiced something one way for years and someone shows you a new way of doing something. This has always been one of the hardest things to overcome as an instructor. I experienced this first hand when I wrote an online article on trigger finger placement. In my article I contended the long-held belief that you must contact the trigger on the middle of the pad at the tip of your trigger finger. Although I gave compelling evidence that there is a better way, I received some negative comments from people who didn't even try the new technique. They fought for their beliefs due to strong cognitive dissonance. So before you read any more, you need to ask yourself which is more important, being a better shooter or sticking to traditions?

Trigger control needs to be maintained throughout the firing sequence, and this can be especially difficult with a pistol. The two main reasons pistols are harder to shoot than rifles are the shorter sight radius and the trigger to weapon weight ratio. Any time your trigger weight is more than the weight of the weapon; you've got your work cut out for you. This is why "race guns" (guns used in competitions) are heavy with light triggers and the guns we shoot in combat are the opposite. So what works for someone with a competition gun shooting paper targets will not work downrange with your government-issued sidearm. Unfortunately, a lot of what is being taught comes from these great range shooters and what works for them. I'm not saying that what they are teaching is wrong, and I'm sure it works with their specially made guns; it just might not be the best technique for combat operations or any off-range shooting you do when you've got to control a tiny trigger with two gallons of adrenaline pumping through your system.

What if you were learning how to drive a race car and your instructor told you all car seats had to be set to the same distance from the steering wheel. It didn't matter how tall you were, your body shape, or if your arms looked like you came from Planet of the Apes. You will keep that seat in the same position! Of course you're going to listen — he's a great driver!

Does this sound right to you? Of course not; but why should

it make sense when a firearms instructor tells you the "law" about where you need to put your finger? Think about all the different sizes, shapes, and strengths of our hands. Look at the finger joints alone of any group of shooters and you'll see they are all in different places. How then can it make sense that they all put their finger on a trigger in the same place and be expected to shoot well? Now think about all the different sizes and shapes of handguns out there and we're all still going to put our finger in the same place?

I know this is going to upset some people. For almost twenty years I too had been told exactly where to put my finger on the trigger and when I first started instructing I was regurgitating the same company line I was told. I would tell students where to put their finger and if it didn't work for them (normally some whining about their hands being "different") I would have them change (weaken) their grip so they could put their finger where they were told. It never worked well and I usually deemed them "bad shooters."

It took a while but I finally took off my blinders and realized you shouldn't adjust 99 percent of where your hand comfortably contacts your gun (grip) so that 1 percent (tip of finger) goes where someone with different size/shaped hands than you told you it works best. If you have an instructor who is telling you where to put your finger, give him the finger! Actually he'll need to give you his finger if he's telling you where you need to put it on the trigger. Your hands are not the same as his (go ahead, look!), so you may need to put your trigger finger somewhere else.

The first thing you need to do for good trigger control is establish a good grip. Once that's done, wherever your finger hits that trigger is the best place for you to put your finger on the trigger of that gun. Different person = different place. Different gun = different place. With the gun comfortably in your hand, you're going to have much better recoil management and better trigger control.

The most important thing is being able to pull the trigger while maintaining correct sight alignment. In the end it doesn't matter how you do it as long as you get it done and can do it quickly and consistently. Anyone who tells you something different is likely more concerned with doing it their way than putting effective fire downrange.

Another thing that I was taught years ago was that you need apply consistent pressure to the trigger until the shot breaks. This seemed to work most of the time, but there were times when someone would move in my path or my tango would move and my shot would break outside of center mass. I realized the problem was the rule I was following; that I had to keep pulling the trigger until the shot broke.

To produce an accurate shot, you need to carry out many tasks simultaneously. This is why it's important not to concentrate on one thing. When you shoot, you need to have an open mind so you can take in all the external stimuli and adjust as needed. If all your concentration is on the front sight, how can you react to other input?

Finally, make sure you press the trigger straight to the rear so you don't pull your shots. If what you're doing now works, then don't change it. But if it's not, give this a try. (Remember, use what works, not what I or anyone else tell you.) Keep the second joint of your trigger finger pointed straight at your target as you press the trigger. By doing so it's nearly impossible to push or pull the shot with your trigger finger. The tip of the finger may work well with a light trigger on a heavy gun, but with a heavy trigger you're much more likely to pull shots when trying to balance the tip of your finger on the trigger. I've used this technique to improve the shooting of many SEAL sniper

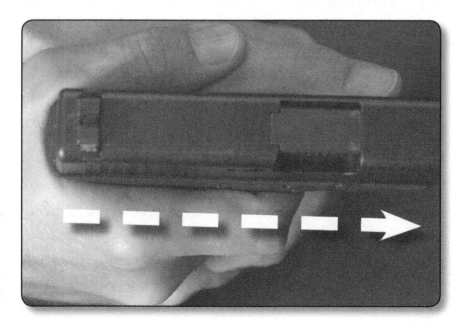

students over the years and if you're contorting your hand all in the name of finger placement, I know it will help you too. Give it a try next time you dry fire (you do dry fire, don't you?) and then try it out on the range.

Another aspect you need to consider is where your finger is vertically along the face of the trigger. The trigger is a lever, just like any other and you need to adjust your finger up or down on the lever to achieve the best mechanical advantage. Lowering your finger just a little bit may give you just enough leverage to achieve a smooth pull without disturbing the sights.

As you press back, the pressure on the trigger needs to come only from the trigger finger. To do this you need to first have a good grip and not let any part of your trigger finger drag along the frame of the gun. Some shooters have a tendency to squeeze the trigger with their whole hand and this will cause the sights to move off target. To train your body to pull the trigger correctly, I recommend dry-fire training.

Start with a weapon that has been cleared and safe. Now establish a proper grip on the gun and sit with the gun in your lap. Practice pulling the trigger like this until you really feel how the trigger moves. You can make major improvements in your trigger pull by doing this because there is nothing else to think about. Once you're comfortable with this, stand up, mount your gun, and do the same thing with your eyes closed. Again, all you need to do is manipulate the trigger without worrying about your sights. After that, do the same thing pointing at a blank wall. It's much easier to see if you're maintaining proper sight alignment on a blank wall than it is looking at a target. Of course the final step is to add in a target.

To fire an effective shot, the pressure on the trigger needs to be smooth and even. This does not mean slow! You can pull the trigger as fast as you want as long as it's smooth. Smooth is fast, but slow is just ... slow. Speed in shooting comes from getting the gun out of the holster, mounted, and your sights aligned on target quickly. If you work on doing these things fast, you can use the extra time for sight refinement and smooth trigger manipulation. I see a lot of guys on the range that take their time getting their gun on target and then start mashing the trigger in an attempt to "shoot fast." Remember to make up time anywhere else than your trigger squeeze!

Go to http://HowToShootLikeANavySEAL.com/videos to register to receive your 12 free training videos.

Since we're on the topic of triggers, let's stay there ... your trigger finger should never leave the face of the trigger during the shooting sequence. I put my finger on the trigger as soon as I can safely do so after identifying my target and the decision to shoot has been made. Normally this is right after my gun is out of the holster and rotated to point at my target. If I need to shoot from the hip I'm ready, if not I'll continue up to fully mount the weapon. My finger will begin moving as soon as my eyes see what they need to see to take the shot.

As I stated earlier, I don't pull the trigger with my finger; I pull it with my eyes. As soon as the shot breaks I pause with the trigger to the rear, normally as the muzzle is coming up. I then let the trigger out only until I feel the sear reset. By this time my muzzle has settled and I have pressure back on the trigger ready to shoot again if needed. This is my follow through, which I will cover in the next chapter. It is only after I have decided I no longer need to deliver exceptional customer service that I take my finger off the trigger.

Again, rather than saying, "Front sight, front sight, front sight," I have a picture in my mind of what I need to see for my finger to move and I pull the trigger with my eyes. If the picture is not there, my finger does not move; but as long as I see that picture my finger will continue to move until the picture changes or the shot breaks. To do this you'll need to practice visual patience. Visual patience means that you don't rush your shot if it's not there.

Let's Review:

1. Start off with a good grip. Don't let the tail wag the dog!

2. Let your finger land naturally on the trigger

3. Consider moving the finger lower on the face of the trigger

4. Keep the middle knuckle of your trigger finger pointed at your target

5. Pull the trigger with your eyes

6. Smooth

7. Keep finger in contact with the trigger

8. Dry fire

Of course if you're not in the process of engaging a target, you need to keep your finger off the trigger. One of the main reasons to not have your finger on the trigger is the body's natural startle response. When we are startled our body naturally contracts muscles and this often leads to unintended discharges if the finger is on the trigger. This could be a bad day if you're pointing your gun at something you weren't willing to destroy.

Follow-Through

A lot of people have a problem with the last fundamental, and not just when it comes to effective shooting. Following-through means seeing what you've started through to the end. For instance, what if I wrote the first five or six chapters of this book, but never wrote the seventh? Lack of follow-through is the reason we can't stand politicians, right? They tell us they're going to do something, but it never happens. When it comes to shooting, you need to finish what you've started too, you need to see each shot through to completion, and my aim is to show you how.

Colonel Jeff Cooper once said, "The best defense against a vicious attack is a more vicious, explosive and overwhelming, offensive counter-attack; followed through to the very end with the attacker being down, disabled, and out of the fight." So following through with each shot we fire means we have to maintain our shooting fundamentals after the shot breaks for a fraction of a second, but it also means we have to follow through with the fight until our enemy is no longer a threat.

I will cover this last point later in the chapter, but let's start out with the marksmanship part of follow-through.

Follow-through is a term that most of us have heard from the first time anyone taught us about marksmanship fundamentals. But it is also one of the most neglected. Maybe because it's last on every list that shooters assume it's the least important, but neglecting the follow-through can negate all the steps you previously took to deliver an accurate shot. Follow-through simply means that you continue to apply all fundamentals of marksmanship after the weapon fires. A proper follow-through allows the weapon to deliver the round precisely on target and recoil in a natural and consistent manner.

To follow through in shooting, you need to do the following:

1. Call the shot (more on this later).

2. Stay relaxed and do not react to the sound or movement of the weapon.

3. Maintain your shooting platform to include head position.

4. Maintain proper grip.

5. Re-acquire sight alignment after your muzzle settles.

6. Continue holding the trigger to the rear for a split second.

7. Re-acquire sight picture.

8. Let out the trigger only until it resets.

9. Prep the trigger for follow-on shots if needed.

Looking at this list you can see that the follow-through is just continuing to employ all the other fundamentals after the gun goes bang and preparing for the next shot if needed. Do not think of the shot breaking as the final step in taking a shot. I see too many guys on the line firing a shot and coming straight back to their retention or low-ready position. If this sounds like you, you're not following through and you'll never master the art of shooting. You know you are actually following through if you can see the muzzle flash in daylight or see the front sight come out of the rear notch.

As you are learning to follow through, do so to the same spot on a static target, but as you get better you'll need to practice lining your sights up to a new place each time. In combat, your target will be moving. If not it's dead and you don't need to waste your ammo.

The first step to a successful follow-through is a proper and consistent grip. The reason the grip is important to follow-through is that it will determine how your gun recoils after the shot. If your grip is not even or consistent, your recoil will vary and your shot placement will not be consistent. Even pressure with your grip means just that, even pressure with both your hands on the gun. If you're trying to grip the gun with different pressures with each hand (i.e. 60/40), the gun will recoil to the side of less resistance and affect your follow-through.

A well-executed follow-through needs to happen after every round you shoot. The math should be pretty simple. However many shots you take, always remember to stay on the target, acquire another sight picture and be ready to take one additional shot. So for example, if you're firing a two-shot string, you need to be ready to take the third shot. I've found this is the best way to ensure a good follow-through. Rather than trying to think about all the steps needed, simply prepare yourself and your gun to fire another shot.

Here's a chart you can print out and take to the range if needed:

Number of actual shots taken	Number of sight pictures
1	2
2	3
3	4
4	5
5	6

Using my patent-pending technique and chart not only gives the bullet the time it needs to exit the barrel while remaining aimed at the intended target, but it also ensures you remain ready to take follow-on shots if necessary. Of course you don't need this chart. All you need to do is remember to follow through on every shot you take.

We've all heard the common expression when it comes to shooting: "Slow is smooth and smooth is fast." I understand what it's trying to point out, but if you're going slow, how can that ever be fast? Sure you need to start off learning things slowly and you can't push your speed past what your current skill level allows, but if you just continue to go slow, that's never going to equal fast. To be able to shoot fast and accurate, you need to be ready to finish your trigger squeeze as soon as your sights settle back down on your intended target. To be able to do this, you need to have a good follow-through by practicing the steps listed above and maintain contact with the trigger at all times.

Speed doesn't come from just doing things faster. It comes from you doing things smoothly and consistently. If your sights are not settling in the same place after each round you shoot, you're going to have to take the time to see where your sights are and then make adjustments before taking the next shot. I like to tell my students that, "Speed happens." If you're trying to increase your speed without the proper techniques to support it, you're going to fumble and make mistakes. This is where we get the saying, "Slow is smooth and smooth is fast." But once you have the proper foundation to support faster shooting, let speed happen.

Regardless of your shooting speed, follow-through is an important fundamental for accurate shooting. Sight alignment and trigger control are the two most important steps in marksmanship and they both need to be maintained during your follow-through. Sight alignment in shooting is more accurately defined as sight refinement and pulling your trigger is better defined as trigger management. You can't just line up the sights once and pull the trigger if you're expecting a good result. Your sight alignment needs to be continually refined and your trigger needs to be active until all threats are neutralized; this means follow-through.

Calling Your Shot

For some reason, many shooters think that calling their shots is reserved only for world-class shooters or snipers. I've found that if you just start doing it, you'll see it's fairly easy and quickly becomes second nature. Calling the shot is also extremely simple, there's just one step: When the shot breaks, remember what the sight picture looked like. By doing so, you should be able to "call" where the impact will be on the target. I tell guys to imagine you're taking a picture with a camera and the trigger is the shutter release button. When the flash goes off (bang), you've got your picture. Also, don't be afraid to call what you see. Many times when I start working with guys on this technique, they just continue to call, "center" shot after shot. They're not hitting center, but are just not nit-picking what they saw. Start practicing calling your shots and you'll be surprised at how quickly your shooting improves.

Finishing the Fight

Although it's not part of marksmanship, making sure you have taken care of all threats is still an important aspect of combat shooting. So to extend your follow-through to any "real-life" shooting scenario, you need to make sure that there are no other threats that require customer service. To do this you need to maintain your awareness not only 360 degrees, but also for any possible threats from above or below. This can be especially challenging in urban and maritime environments.

Just like every other fundamental of shooting, you need to practice scanning for threats and checking on your teammates, family, or bystanders every time you shoot to make it a habit. If you don't practice on the range, you won't do it in a gunfight, and it could cost you your life. Doing a good scan also helps to break your body alarm response and open up any tunnel vision you're having and trust me, we all have it.

To properly scan, do the following:

1. Do a good follow-through and be prepared to take another shot if needed. If you've determined that the target is no longer a threat, move on to step two.

2. Take your finger off the trigger and bring it to a safe, tactical ready position.

3. Do a 360-degree scan for additional threats. This does not mean just shaking your head from left to right, it means really seeing and assessing what's around you. If there are people around you, look at their hands. Get off the X! Quickly assess your environment for any available cover and move to it if it makes tactical sense. Often this is not possible on a range, but practice thinking about where you could go. Again, don't just look; see and assess!

4. Turn your head to either the left or the right. If you know which direction there is a higher probability of threats, you should turn that way first. It's important to see all the way behind you and to accomplish this, tilt your head down slightly. By doing so, you will open up your field of view by as much as sixty degrees. (During the scan, make sure you are also looking for any threats that might be either above or below the level you're on.) Also, don't be afraid to move your feet to scan 360. A lot of

guys I work with are told never to move their feet or that their feet need to always be pointed downrange. If this is you, break that habit and see what you need to see. Just make sure you keep your weapon pointed straight down in an inside-carry position so you don't point it at anything you do not want to shoot!

5. Now look back at your original threat and make sure it's still down. Did he have on body armor and now he's getting back up? He may be asking for seconds.

6. Turn the opposite direction from where you originally checked, again making sure you look behind, above and below you.

7. Finally, look back again at your original threat to make sure it's still down.

Always expect more threats. If there was one threat, be prepared for two; if there are two threats, be prepared for three, and so on. After your scan, make sure you know the condition of your weapon and plus-up as needed.

Practicing these combat fundamentals with every shot you take is the only way to master the art of shooting. And just like anything in life, if you don't follow through, your previous work is wasted.

Mission Planning

As shooters, our range time is very valuable in more ways than one. At most ranges it costs money just to shoot. On top of that you have to buy targets, ammo, and weapon cleaning supplies ... the list adds up quickly. But I haven't even mentioned the most important thing you have ... time. My time is very valuable to me so I am not going to waste it when I have the opportunity to advance my skill-set. I know a lot of people when they go to the range just say, "Hey, I'm gonna go shootin'!" They go to the range, set up a target and start shooting; and they keep shooting until they're out of ammo or they run out of time (there it is again). Even if you say you're going to practice, what does that really mean? To me it means nothing but wasted range time unless you have a well laid out plan.

Before your next trip to the local gun-slinging establishment, have an idea of what you want to train before you get there. You might want to work on some different stances, grip, trigger control, follow-through, or anything else you need work on. I believe strongly in Weakness-Biased Training. Weakness-Biased Training means that you take a serious look at the chinks in your armor and work at correcting them. We all have weaknesses in our shooting, and that's where you need to spend the majority of your time. Once you've fixed these things, there will be something else you need to work on. It's an endless cycle that you need to continue as long as your goal is improved performance.

The point I want to drive home is to have a plan and stick to it. It's best to actually write out your plan in your range book. When you get to the range, just go down the list. When you're done, write down how your training went and what else you need to work on next time you're at the range or your next dry-fire training session. Dry-fire training is the single best thing you can do to improve your shooting. You don't go to the range and just bust caps to get better. Live fire just confirms all the dry firing that you've been doing.

Most of us don't have access to endless ammo. When I was in the SEAL Teams we had unlimited supplies of ammunition and it was great! There is no way I could have bought all that ammo. But even with all that ammo, I dry fired all the time ... and still do. Every great shooter dry fires A LOT; it's what makes them great! If you want to be great too, remember, dry fire every day for fifteen to twenty minutes and practice weakness-biased training.

Point blank: When you go to the range, don't waste your ammo, don't waste your time; know what your weakness are and write down a training plan.

Training plan: _____

_____

_____

_____

_____

_____

_____

_____

_____

_____

_____

_____

_____

So Now What?

Whenever people ask me how they can Shoot Like a Navy SEAL, I always say the same thing: Train your ass off! That's the short answer. I never mention any particular technique or even the fundamentals of combat marksmanship I went over in this book. Nope, what you need to do is train. Sure there are plenty of other great little tricks out there and I'm always trying to acquire new tools for my toolbox, but no matter what skill or technique I'm working on, I'm ... well ... working. By reading this book you now have the knowledge to be an accurate combat shooter. You just need to apply yourself or this knowledge will go to waste. Everyone is looking for the one trick to make them a better shooter, but one thing that's never changed is what it takes to be a great gunfighter: hands-on training.

But as we push on into the information age, the way many people view what is considered "training" is changing. I've noticed a disturbing trend lately when I talk to people about firearms training. I'm finding many people are no longer willing to put in the hard work needed to learn the art of warfare since it would be much easier to just buy the latest training book or training video. Then all they have to do is kick back on the couch with a few cool ones and train! Don't get me wrong, I've got no beef with getting more information or learning how to do something through a shooting book or video. There are some great ones out there, including this one of course! But the caveat is, once you've got the information, you need to use it. Don't just sit there like a wallflower … skin that smoke wagon and do a little ballet with that boom-stick.

So what does this mean for you? Well, if your training is already as good as you want it to be, you don't need to do anything. But if you want to improve your skills, you can't just sit around waiting for the next "Dyno-Reflexive Combat-Carbine" video to come out so you can improve those mad-ninja skills. It means you should take the information you already have or just got from this book to the range and see where your skill level is. Milk the knowledge you've already got for all it's worth and if you get to a point where your training is stagnating, then hop back online and order away! But if you're hammering the basics and really working to be the weapon, this journey in self-mastery will not soon end. Even when you get to the point that you think you've mastered the basics, just remember that advanced shooting is just the basics done smoother and faster.

There are two things involved in firearms training. One is a weapon and one is a tool.

Which one are you going to be?

Go to **ChrisSajnog.com** for my free firearms training newsletter or to learn more about my online training programs.

Printable Card: Navy SEAL Combat Marksmanship Fundamentals

Print this page, cut out and take to the range.

Navy SEAL Fundamentals of Combat Marksmanship

1. Establish a good <u>shooting platform</u>.
2. Establish a solid <u>grip</u> on the weapon.
3. Align the <u>sights</u> perfectly and continuously.
4. Place your sights on the <u>target</u>.
   ### - Focus on front sight!
5. <u>Breathe</u> normally — don't hold your breath.
6. Control the <u>trigger</u> with your eyes.
7. <u>Follow through</u> on every shot.

How to Shoot Like a Navy SEAL

- Always shoot with a positive attitude.

- Have an open mind.

- Have a plan.

- Train every day.

- Train to your weaknesses.

- Dry fire.

- Use a range book.

Range Safety Rules

1. Treat every gun as if it were loaded.

2. Keep your finger off the trigger until ready to shoot.

3. Always keep gun pointed in a safe direction.

4. Be sure of your target as well as the foreground and background.

5. Know the range rules.

About the Author

Chris is a retired Navy SEAL Chief Petty Officer, Master Firearms Instructor, Neural-Pathway Training (NPT) Expert, public speaker, and a Disabled Veteran Small Business Owner. Chris commands an unparalleled level of respect when it comes to firearms and tactical training. He was hand-selected to develop the curriculum for the US Navy SEAL Sniper training program. As a Navy SEAL he was the senior sniper instructor, a certified Master Training Specialist (MTS), BUD/S, and advanced training marksmanship instructor.

After retiring from the SEAL Teams in 2009, Chris began training civilians and law enforcement officers. He has a passion for finding innovative ways to teach elite-level shooting skills as fast as possible to his clients and delivering personalized training online.

Chris lives in San Diego, CA, with his wife, Laura, and their two boys, Caden and Owen.

To contact the author or to sign up for his free training newsletter, go to **http://chrissajnog.com**

Navy SEAL Shooting

Learn everything you need to know about mental training, marksmanship, malfunctions, movement, manipulations and mastery from one of the most respected firearms instructors in the world, US Navy SEAL firearms instructor Chris Sajnog.

Navy SEAL Shooting is the culmination of Chris' twenty-five years of elite firearms instructor experience training the worlds most elite warriors. It covers several secret shooting skills you can't find anywhere else. With hundreds of pictures and diagrams showing you each technique, it's like having your own personal Navy SEAL Instructor.

Go to **http://navysealshooting.com**
to continue your learning.

Notes: _____

_____

_____

_____

_____

_____

_____

_____

_____

_____

_____

_____

_____

_____

_____

Made in the USA
Monee, IL
17 December 2023

49697192R00083